MW00880395

Cancer Is So Limited

And Other Poems of Faith

By Robert L. Lynn

ISBN 13 978-148 2074826

The author is especially indebted to these
colleagues in the Georgia Poetry Society, all
accomplished writers and leaders in Georgia poetry,
who read the manuscript and gave valued counsel:

Sandy Hokanson
Alpharetta, Georgia

Jill Jennings
Woodstock, Georgia

John K. Ottley, Jr.
Alpharetta, Georgia

Ronald W. Self
Columbus, Georgia

Steven O. Shields
Johns Creek, Georgia

Dedicated to my talented and loving children:

Susan Lynn Calonkey

Christopher Moore Lynn

"Poetry allows the human soul to speak."

—-*Carolyn Forche'*

"Poetry is a way of taking life by the throat."

—-*Robert Frost*

Contents

Contents *(continued)*

Contents (continued)

VII

Foreward

Because faith long has been central to my life, my third book of poetry focuses on poems of the spirit. Of the 400 verses I have penned, about 70 have religious themes. Besides collecting many of those into this volume I have created 25 new poems in which the poet talks (in some cases argues) with God regarding some of the pivotal and demanding "requirements" of the Christian faith.

I suspect that many who will explore the poems have struggled with some of the same questions in their own faith pilgrimages.

I hope that each reader will be drawn to a deeper understanding of, and relationship with, his or her God.

For more information about the poetry, background and poetic endeavors of the author, welcome to my poetry web site at www.robertllynn.com

Robert L. Lynn
January, 2013
Duluth, Georgia

The Title Poem:
A Life of Its Own

By far my most famous poem is *Cancer Is So Limited*, also known as *What Cancer Cannot Do*. It was written in a midnight burst of inspiration to comfort and encourage a dear friend who was sentenced to death by cancer. After giving it to him, I almost forgot about the verse, which took on a life of its own. Someone confiscated it, brazenly attributed it to Anonymous, and hundreds of millions copied it and used it to give hope to friends who were cancer victims, or to sell it as calligraphy, plaques and other forms without attribution or compensation.

Some oncologists even quote it on the back of their business cards. A woman claimed it on her new web site
as her philosophy of life as she battled the disease. A musical therapist has distributed it to her patients and set it to music.

When I last Googled it I received over **167,000,000 hits!**

I am thrilled that the verse undoubtedly lends encouragement to millions of cancer patients and wish that the influence of the poem will continue to expand across the earth in many languages

The legal messages framed by my copyright attorney are: 1- Anyone who wants to use the poem in whole or in part must have my permission. (contact me at robertllynn@comcast.net or 770-876-2904) and must include the wording: Copyright 2007 by Robert L. Lynn.
2 — Sale of any product containing all or part of the poem will require permission and a contract.

On the next page is the copyrighted verse.

Cancer Is So Limited

They've sentenced you with invisible cells that
    secret themselves deep in body recesses and multiply
    lymphatic assault on vital functions.

Can cancer conquer you?
    I doubt it, for the strengths I see in you
    have nothing to do with cells and blood and muscle.

For cancer is so limited---
    It cannot cripple love.
    It cannot shatter hope.
    It cannot corrode faith.
    It cannot eat away peace.
    It cannot destroy confidence.
    It cannot kill friendship.
    It cannot shut out memories.
    It cannot silence courage.
    It cannot invade the soul.
    It cannot reduce eternal life.
    It cannot quench the spirit.
    It cannot cancel resurrection.

Can cancer conquer you?
    I doubt it, for the strengths I see in you
    have nothing to do with cells and blood and muscle.

I

All Truth

*"But when he, the Spirit of truth, comes,
he will guide you into all truth."*
— John 16:13a (NIV)

I can't get past
those red-letter words Jesus spoke—
The promise is all bold,
only a divine could have etched it.
The fountain of truth —
all truth, not fragments —
all truth the Teacher will teach,
the wisdom of the Christ,
all truth, All Truth, ALL TRUTH —
too rich a bounty to neglect.
Exulting,
I begin to comprehend,
to gather
                    ALL.

God-Spurning

Man has the inalienable right
to spurn God any time and place.
But one must be a simpleton
who rejects God over and again,
not seeing he's like the patient
with recurring staph
who declines antibiotics;
or the woman knotted with guilt
but won't tack the heading to forgiveness;
one whose soul is shriveling
who won't swallow the golden nutrient;
or who drifts like a swept log
but brushes off the gift of a God-compass;
who can never get on with people
but passes up inviting a loving Christ into his heart;
who hoists all his stresses alone,
refusing the elevating prayers of believers.

However, he can pivot any moment
to embrace the grace he's shunned.
For all the while, with arms thrown wide,
Jesus beckons the God-spurner,
"Come unto me, you tired,
and I will give you rest."

Lasting Fruit

*"You did not choose me, but I chose you and appointed you
to go and bear fruit—fruit that will last."* — John 15:16 (NIV)

If I had been God
I never would have left
the winning of the world
to mortals like you and me.
Rather I may have stirred
a magic potion
to effect forgiveness
for the weight of guilt and sin.
Or made a Matterhorn
one could scale
to peace of mind.

But, Lord, your charge is
as clear as a mountain pool
to those of us
who follow after you,
to bear you fruit that lasts.
You trust our voices,
our feet with your gospel,
next door and to earth's ends.
And since you didn't inquire
how I would draw
your kingdom blueprint,
I figure we least likely witnesses
had best hew to task,
in your Spirit's strength,
if we are to harvest
your eternal fruit.

No Greater Love

Jesus was ever-trying to illumine truth
for his dense disciple band:

*"No greater love can anyone show
than to lay down his life for his friends."*

Just before he placed his life
on the cross at Golgotha
for his friends and for their wrongs,
he emblazoned this inscription
down the passages of time,
never to be rescinded:

*"Love each other as I love you;
be willing to sacrifice for one another
as I am poised to give my life for you."*

I order you, like soldiers on the battlefield,
be primed to give last blood
for the faithful, and for me.
This I require, this I **command....***

*John 15:13

Redeeming the Time

*"See then that ye walk circumspectly,
not as fools, but as wise, redeeming
the time..."* —Ephesians 5:15-16a
(KJV)

This day may be all I have,
let me walk it wisely.
I exist without yesterday's minutes,
nor can I standtimedead tomorrow
to paint or trowel over errors.
I must live this platinum day,
not with my sinewed muscles alone
but as his breath enobles each hour.
It's later than ever before;
I must redeem the evaporating seconds,
treading wisely....before dark.

Talking Points

We could chat about how to lose your slicing drive,
or text a choice recipe for trendy, moistest cake,
or herald the IPO sure as ivy to grow,
the med trumpeted to induce sleep,
the cell number of my quick, expert handyman,
the vacation adventure my kids savored,
the novel these hands wouldn't put down,
the movie which left me reeling.

OR

I could point out how I accepted eternal life
from the Holy One who sacrificed his Son,
the wellspring of peace and comfort,
for you and for me.
That other talk is drivel beside
this certified Hallelujah News.

The Center

"But seek first his kingdom and his
righteousness". — Matthew 6:33 (NIV)

Not my favorite command from Jesus' lips,
an asphalt scrape against my priorities,
my organizational center of life,
my racing after cultural prizes.
The unambiguous Lord:
"Kingdom first, and his righteousness,"
no wink of eye,
no excusing this or that disciple.
At this instant the pivot of my life is "me;"
the kingdom hovers as vapor beyond my sightline.
But if I stake His kingdom first,
God will inhabit my center,
investing my life with worth,
and as a bonus layering daily
what my existence requires.
"My kingdom first" --
the hardest (and choicest) mandate
to leave my Savior's mouth.

Worry

Worrying
Is not your thing,
Will only clog your way.

Borrow not
Tomorrow's blots;
Don't let them foil today.

Fretting, slow,
Be anxious, no;
Your fears God will allay.

II

Burning Hearts

Luke 24:13-35

We slouch along our Emmaus road
of grief as we mourn the Lord,
our hopes side-pierced by a Roman spear.

A stranger joins us
as our sandals drag the path,
our future as empty as a cracked water pot.
But with his presence our steps spring,
energy edges back;
his soft tones calm.
He recites prophet's words,
how Messiah had to bleed and die;
our chilled souls warm.

At the fork we beg,
"Stay with us ere day is done."
Reclining, he breaks the bread
and crumbles joyous morsels
for our famished spirits —
we forget our dark dread,
our cataracts fall.
We see the Lord himself
resurrected, at our table, smiling.
Then, like a vapor, he vanishes
leaving us with hearts
still smoking.

Mary Turning

*He appeared first to Mary Magdalene, out of whom
he had driven seven demons. She went and told those
who had been with him and who were mourning and
weeping.*—Mark 16:9-10 (NIV)

All Mary sees now is the empty tomb,
and she cannot go home to Magdala
where Jesus had unbound her
from the seven demons
and her abode in a bone cave.
She can't retreat to nothingness
and life without the miracle-doer.

She spins from the empty sepulchre
as the gardener whispers, "Mary."
"Rabboni", she answers. Jesus teaches her
the first lesson of her new creation:
I am now everywhere,
I cannot be stilled by death;
I am in you, and you in me.
I have slain your devils,
and you do not have to go back
to those foul catacombs.
Keep turning, Mary.

He will also come to us,
exorcise our demons,
and shape us baby-new in him.

Lazarus

Christ can't accept that he is gone,
Although our brother reeks by now;
If only we weren't left alone.

Four days we weep aloud and moan,
To stanch our grief we know not how;
Christ can't accept that he is gone.

Jairus' child's restoring known,
Blind man healed upon His vow;
If only we weren't left alone.

Our loved one wrapped, anointed, prone,
Grave clothing tight, no hopes allow;
Christ can't accept that he is gone.

He owns the might of heaven's throne,
A thousand angels to Him bow;
If only we weren't left alone.

"Come forth," he shouts at tomb of stone,
The bound one walking, death laid low;
Christ won't accept that he is gone,
Now man need never live alone.

Samuel

My barren mother's womb God did restore,
Acceding to her prayer to grant a son.
At three my life was lent at temple door
To help insure the holy work was done.
I grew in favor both with God and man
When poverty of vision cursed the day.
That night I heard my name called out and ran
To Eli, who on third try bade me say,
"Speak, Lord, for now thy humble servant hears."
Then God proclaimed to me his holy vow:
"I'll do a thing through you to tingle ears,
Establish you my promised prophet now."
And I emerged God's spokesman for his day
Because I bent to holy breath alway.

Teresa

I could not vote for beatification of Mother Teresa—
but if I had, and if I had known
that her faith sometimes faltered,
and, depressed, she feared her life was a waste,
that her feeble deeds were never enough,
she seldom sensed God's presence—
I would still be inclined to vote for her
because I'm dubious of faultless saints,
those ignorant of their own shortcomings,
who can't imagine God employing clay feet,
can't countenance doubters,
like Job, Jeremiah, Paul, and Jesus.
I'll wager they won't rescind Teresa's sainthood,
but if, if, if . . . perchance another test were sanctioned,
and if, miraculously, I sat on the panel, I would cast boldly
this Protestant's ballot for Saint Teresa of Calcutta.

The Queen Who Saved Her People

The king chose comely Esther as his queen,
But he knew not she was of Jewish stem,
Nor that her people faced a kingdom purge —
Haman-fueled—he thought her race a scourge
And led the king to sound their mourning dirge.
But Esther staked her life, approached the king,
Aware her death his wave could bring,
Was granted royal right to ask one thing:
The king loved Esther, and he freely gave
Protection for the Israelite enclave.
Queen Esther knew divinity had brought
Her to the kingdom for this act so brave.
And Haman died upon the gallows wrought
For Jews; God's care for chosen thus was taught.

The Wall Is Down

1981

In Jericho the subjects sleep,
Secure behind their fortress steep;
Joshua's forces in early morn,
Circling with ark and priestly horn,
Shout in strength of Jehovah's crown;
The wall is down, the wall is down.

In Bethlehem in longing state
For Emmanuel the faithful wait;
Could it be that Israel's God
Would ever walk this human sod?
But heaven stooped to tiny town;
The wall is down, the wall is down.

In Jerusalem the elements rage,
Zion's temple on center stage;
The ancient veil, impenetrable zone
Twixt sinful man and Holy One;
The curtain rends at Golgotha's sound;
The wall is down, the wall is down.

In garden tomb the corpse is still
For death has cast its final chill;
Man's Saviour lies with pierced side,
With him both hope and peace have died;
But, lo, the body can't be found!
The wall is down, the wall is down.

In Eastern Bloc the millions reel
From forty years of curtained steel;
In men's breasts sweet freedom's wind,
Creator-born, can never end.
It blows to ruins the concrete mound;
The wall is down, the wall is down.

Whatnot Faith

"Jesus replied, "I tell you the truth, if you have faith and do not doubt, not only can you do what was done to the fig tree, but also you can say to this mountain, 'Go, throw yourself into the sea,' and it will be done. If you believe, you will receive whatever you ask for in prayer."—

Matthew 21:21-22 (NIV)

Lazy on the daybed
one steamy August high noon,
cooled a mere four degrees
by the farm home's lone water fan,
the boy's green Gideon New Testament
having just intrigued me with
Jesus' promise that, if I pray
to move a mountain
without an ounce of doubt,
the hill will straightway
be plopped into the sea.

No peaks near Fox, Oklahoma,
but I did spy high in a corner
my Mother's whatnot shelf
bearing the tiny Grecian vase.
Eyes clinched, I begged
"Lord, let a five dollar bill
be in the urn, the one
with oxen circling round.
I BELIEVE it's folded there,
*I really, really do **BELIEVE** it's there."*

(Continued)

(Continued)

Poor etiquette, I knew,
to faith-test the whatnot shelf.
I coolly waited two slow minutes,
tip-toed to the corner,
commandeered a ladder-backed chair,
lowered the vase and squinted
into the empty chamber,
reset it reverently,
and ran outside to romp
in the shade with my dog.

III

A Prayer for Students

God, I pray for these lives
  made in your image,
who came to this campus
  where Christ is Lord
  to sit at your feet
  and gather your wisdom.
In your name and on their behalf
  I pray that you shall grant:

not that they will be the best
  but that they will do their best;
not a 4.0 average on our scale
  but a 4.0 average on your scale;
not freedom from struggle
  but growth amidst struggle;
not the absence of pressure
  but strength to endure pressure;
 not the bestowal of new gifts
  but to hone those you've already given;
not to gain merely the wisdom of men,
  but to access the vault of the wisdom of Christ;
not that they be sheltered from truth
  but that they be guided into all truth;
not all-American honor and acclaim
  but reverence for your holy name;
not more training in receiving,
  teach them, Lord, the art of giving;
not with surface, selfish, childish love
  but knowledge-passing Jesus' love;
 not the drive to be served by all
  but, like your Son, to become servants of all.

AMEN

Altar on Lynndale Place

That first house we built:
three bedrooms, two baths, half-city view,
fireplace, balcony,
and an altar made up
of a Bible rest and a Holman's Head of Christ.
Only a young family's resolve
that home worship and devotion to God
belonged, like bedrock, in our blueprints.
I wonder what the buyers six years later
surmised of our simple sanctum.
Our current home holds no such shrine,
and experience may have taught us a core truth about altars:
to survive the elements they must be framed in the heart.

Faith Search

I retreated Saturday with the college gang to Acadia camp.
In steamy room
    rapt students pressed the perpetual quest:
    "where is God's path for me?"

On back row I sensed the sweaty struggle
    as freshman map-readers
        examined crossroads,
        grappled with signs;
    upperclassmen traced their brief forays
        into unknown,
        uncharted land.

I smiled: decades back
    I voiced the same question,
    felt the incessant gnawing,
    switched my major, once, then twice;
    doubt still clung.

Lord, please, don't let these seekers miss
    these ventures toward faith,
    the thrill of search,
    the mystery of seeing your will unfold
        from blind uncertainty.

Freshman's Fear

This new semester glares at me,
  each Monday, Wednesday, Friday
    at 8, 10, and 1,
    and Tuesday, Thursday
      at 9:25 and 12:45,
  the clock compels my presence,
    and I'm on the edge of fear.
New teacher, packed class, brainy kids
  who spit out answers like Google.
  And I wonder,
    " what am I doing here?
  Will I survive a month, mid-term?
    Can I cope, compete?
  Oh, God, is it possible
    I'm not college material?"

But today at last the professor's jumble
  made some sense.
  "I'm starting to comprehend,
    I read that last night."
  A smile spreads inside my mind.
    "I think I'm catching on!
  Maybe I'm not so dense after all.
  Hey, me, I'm learning!"

Mind Transplant

"Let this mind be in you which was also in Christ Jesus."— Philippians 2:5 (KJV)

I know only one way to go about
heeding the Apostle's admonition.
I cannot by steel will
appropriate the cerebrum of the Christ of Galilee,
or be shocked into divine mentality.
The only path I know to Jesus-mindedness
is to act as he did, breathe his words,
follow his sight lines,
assume his attitudes,
yield to his allegiances,
love the multitudes and weep,
CAT-scan the hearts of people,
bow to the Father's plan,
tune in the wails of outcasts, the maimed,
pull aside to commune with the Father,
poise to spill my blood for friends,
uncowed by demonic power,
bent upon proclaiming God's Kingdom,
arms flung open to the Spirit,
as the holy graft
takes root in me.

Proverbs on Christian Teachers

A paraphrase of Proverbs 31:10-30

Who can assess the value of Christian teachers,
for their worth is far, far above the wages
and the stature they command.
The hearts of their administrators safely trust in them.
They will do good and not evil all the semesters of their lives.
They seek books, maps, videos, and online resources.
They are like the search engines:
they bring wisdom from afar.
They rise while it is yet night and prepare
     their presentations with diligence,
that their students may be able to compete in a complex world.
They consider a field of knowledge and buy a part thereof;
with the fruit of their hands they spend a life of service therein...
They clothe themselves with faith
     and strengthen their arms with prayer.
They know that education at the feet of Christ is good,
and greatly to be prized among the schools of learning.
They lay their intellect to mold character, values and integrity;
they prepare seekers to live abundantly, and to die victoriously.

(Continued)

(Continued)

They stretch out their hands to the poorer students;
yea, they reach forth to those strugglers
    in whom their Lord sees promise.
They fear not the evil that will confront their students;
for the tapestries of their pupils' lives are being woven
    with strong threads of moral fiber.
Behold, they are living sacrifices of principle, honesty, and
    dedication, and are worthy to be emulated,
for these teachers point learners to God, who is eternal.
High standards and gentle concern are their qualities,
and they exult in the hope that is in Christ Jesus.
They know highest wisdom is in the "teacher come from
God."
Their educational model is him who said, "I am…the truth."
They call not their students servants but friends;
they even give up their evenings for them.
And their students grow up and call them blessed.
Many teachers have taught brilliantly, but you,
O Christian teacher, excels them all,
for you share in the mission and ministry of the kingdom.
Scholarly awards are excellent, and Nobel prizes are coveted;
but teachers who stand beneath the cross,
they shall be praised and emulated.

Self-Architect

Some sages hold that fate has preset
   what I am to be;
by some odd twist of genes and place
   my personhood is cast,
and my volition in the matter of my life
   is minus zero.

But I have learned from the school of life
   that I shape the person I will become;
I do have sway.
Stacked before me are bricks of choice
   that plant the contours of the house I construct.

   I can scale above my environment.
   I can express my thoughts of soul.
   I can opt to lead, or teach, or sell, or sing.
   I can discipline myself.
   I can build self-reliance.
   I can traverse the route to love.
   I can clasp divine hands.
   I can be my own architect.

Brick by brick and wall by wall
   I can build for me a self.

IV

Birmingham Jail

On your birthday I clutch the bars of the cell
behind which you scrawled the famed letter
that turned me around four decades back.

White southern Protestant journalist,
I aimed each dawn to honor God,
taught Sunday school, sang tenor in the choir,

yet thought marches, boycotts, sit-ins
excessive, bad etiquette, ill-timed,
disruptive, and generally rude,

until I opened *The Christian Century*
to your comeback to Birmingham clergy
who lectured protestors: "Negotiate," "Wait."

No "agitator," you heard Macedonian call
to come over and help, since "injustice anywhere
is a threat to justice everywhere."

Unjust laws, you judged, should be resisted,
as did Shadrach, Meshach, Abednego,
and colonial patriots in Boston harbor.

Freedom's stumbling block, you argued,
not only the sheeted Klansmen but also
shepherds of the white congregations.

(Continued)

(Continued)

You freely wore the extremist label
like Old Testament Prophet Amos, and Paul,
and the One who bore the cross for love.

You couldn't quite explain to your little girl
why she never could enter Funtown
as did my nine-year-old Susy.

One reading and my blinders fell
as I felt the laser of your prison pen,
acknowledged the rightness of your cause.

I never marched with you, but, thereafter,
sure inside my soul your case was right,
your pleas just, urgent—now my own.

The sacred cell in which you wrote
is carpeted now with dollar bills,
and through the bars I humbly flutter mine.

Christmas Eve in Henryetta

The band of ice shuttered the interstate;
we slid off at little Henryetta
in front of America's Best Value Inn
and booked the last vacancy,
unable to reach our waiting, worried family.
Thus commenced the interminable night of toasty naps,
vending snacks, and the live telecast from Temple Square
of the Mormon Tabernacle Choir.

As "Angels from the Realms of Glory" pealed
I lifted the plaid window curtain
to uncommonly bright and swirling snow
as the young couple skidded up in their green Volvo
and occupied the rustic tool shed
across the motel drive.

After midnight I spotted three guys
on their Harleys, smoking and genuflecting
outside the shed, their furry caps
mounding like shimmering crowns,
their faces cast as if they'd
just witnessed a roadside miracle.

We drifted back to family dreams
and next day rolled on crusty I-40
to celebrate with our loved ones
the birth two millennia back
in an animal cave in David's town
of Christ the Lord, Emmanuel,
when some travelers like us
commandeered the only room left
with a window open to wonder.

I Am Not Free

I am not free
if my brother is bound—
his fetters also shackle my wrists;
his oppression clamps my ankles,
his rise from bondage
is an updraft for me.
My pillow knows no calm
until my sister owns liberty;
we stroll freedom's walk
together,
        or not at all.

Sacred Place

I pledged months back
with a pilgrim band
to cross this threshold weekly
to pray as one
for us and others,
the congregation
and the world.
And in that span
this ordinary space
has taken on hues
only seen in the heavens:
a tone of possibility,
a shade of community,
a tint of sharing,
a surround of peace,
the white of wings,
the brush of unbundling,
the flush of victory.
And over time
this common chamber
to which I'm drawn
by divine magnet
has metamorphosed into
the Sacred Place.

Slowdown

As a senior stereotyped by church culture
to relax at discipleship, step back,
execute faith less daringly—
I can't square that with
"Ye shall be my witnesses,"
"Seek first God's kingdom,"
"You're the light of the world,"
"Do all to the glory of God."
No power clutching
in the diaconate or in his vineyard,
just heeding Christ,
rejecting like junk bonds
retirement from his commands,
never downsizing his expectations,
ever stretching to love Him
until and through my final breath.

Stoning Pagans

Kids shouldn't hurl stones at pagans in your land,
especially when they're guests
who crossed continents to help you heal from war.
Don't you know that Jesus the Prophet
implored you to love even enemies?
Besides, how will you ever win a person
to your creed if you label him "pagan"
and shell him with missiles?

What game is this that impels a child
to sling gravel at jogging visitor?
Which parent would let a child
hurl pebbles at total strangers?

I wish I spoke the Somali tongue
so I could toss peace words
to kids who cast stones at pagans

*The poet served in the summer of 1998
as a UNICEF educational consultant
to the government of Somaliland.

V

God's Grace

"The grace of our Lord was poured out on me abundantly, along with the faith and the love that are in Christ Jesus."—I Timothy 1:14 (NIV)

What can I count upon
To aid my woeful case?
To lift my weight of guilt,
To bear my sin? *God's Grace.*

Just what will compensate
For acts I would erase?
For errant thoughts, shirked deeds,
Recalcitrance? *God's Grace.*

Never, Lord, allow me
To fall into ungrace;
Show by your example
The rightness of *God's Grace.*

And what helps me to know
In each event and place
The right response the Lord
Prefers I make? *God's Grace.*

What assures my pardon
When standing face to face
With heaven's righteous judge?
God's grace, *God's grace, God's Grace.*

I Love My Church

May be sung to Hymn Tune, *Angel's Story* (O Jesus I Have Promised)

I love my Church, her mission:
To win to him each one,
To teach them his commandments,
Experience the Son;
I love my Church, his own bride,
For her success he stood,
For her he gave his own self,
For her he shed his blood.

I love my Church, her people
Find comfort in distress,
And food for growth and nurture,
Rich fellowship to bless;
I love my Church, her service
Fulfils my deepest needs,
A channel for my giving,
Ennobling all my deeds.

I love my Church, her future,
His power her guarantee,
He shall return to claim her
For all eternity;
I love my Church, her leader
Shows me how I should live;
And as he died for his bride,
To her myself I give.

Lead My Life, Lord

Sing to hymn tune, *Fill My Cup, Lord*, by Richard Blanshard

Like a plane without its radar I was drifting,
No valid purpose could I see;
And then I heard the Savior bidding,
"Take up your cross and daily follow me."

CHORUS:
Lead my life now,
My life is yours now,
Jesus, give me meaning for my days;
Grace sufficient, guide me as I trust in you,
Lead my life,
I yield it up
And follow you.

Like a team without a mission I was wandering,
No useful person could I be;
And then I heard the Savior saying,
"I came to bring you life abundantly."

Like a journey with no end I was aimless;
No worthy future could I know;
And then I heard the Savior promise,
 "My spirit leads you everywhere you go."

Since the time he won my heart my life's had focus;
Each day I aim to do his will;
My prize, eternity with Jesus,
But each hour on earth with him a thrill.

My Backyard Swing

I steal on this day to my backyard swing
As avian choir rehearses to sing;
My silent approach as family naps
Is foiled by my dog's irreverent yaps.

Young squirrels make a maypole of giant oak,
This congregation is fun-loving folk;
Pink roses shout Selahs, defying gloom.
Azaleas weren't told it's too late to bloom.

As I move to and fro, Lord, please draw nigh
To this cathedral with windows of sky;
I'm sure those problems that this day will bring
Can be prayed to size in my backyard swing.

Private Worship

"Thy word is a lamp unto my feet, and a light unto my path."—Psalm 119:105 (KJV)

Six weeks I resided in Islamic land,
unable openly to voice my faith,
watched believers forbidden to assemble;
Catholic dome a plastered tomb.

And so the Christians of Somaliland,
like the faithful huddled in Roman catacombs,
clandestinely worship their Holy God,
personal petitions rise heavenward.
They pore quietly over "lamp to their feet"
as x-ray Spirit pierces roofs and walls.

I concur with Mohammed: faith cannot be forced.
The millisecond it is, authenticity is sacrificed.

**The poet spent the summer of 1998 as a
UNICEF educational consultant to the
government of Somaliland*

Thanksgiving Is My Heart's Cry

May Be Sung to Hymn Tune: *Aurelia*, by Samuel S. Wesley, 1810-1876

Thanksgiving is my heart's cry
To creator of earth,
The author of salvation,
The fountain of new birth.
My grateful spirit swelling
In never-ending praise,
To God, my full devotion,
To you my anthems raise.

Thanksgiving is my heart's cry
For worlds your hands have made,
For firmaments and mountains,
For seas and fields arrayed.
All hail within my being
For gifts of food and life,
For family and friendships
And living free from strife.

Thanksgiving is my passion
For home of liberty,
For nature's rich endowment
From sea to teeming sea.
The blessings of your bounty
I pray be on our land,
Our knees are bent in reverence,
And in your strength we stand.

(Continued)

(Continued)

Thanksgiving is my heart's cry
To one who makes things new,
The framer of the future,
Whose promises prove true.
All gratitude to Jesus
For home prepared for me
With angels and my loved ones,
With God eternally.

We'll Be a Voice

Based on traditional spiritual; may be recited as voice choir.

Who'll be a voice for Christ Jesus,
Who'll sing praises to my Lord?

Who'll be a rep for Christ Jesus,
Who'll be a witness for my Lord?

Who'll write a poem for Christ Jesus,
Who'll testify for my Lord?

Who'll live a life for Christ Jesus,
Who'll show love for my Lord?

Who'll offer all to Christ Jesus,
Give all the credit to my Lord?

Who'll die a witness for Christ Jesus,
Who'll go to glory to live with him?

**We'll be a voice for Christ Jesus,
We'll sing praises to our Lord!**

**We'll be a rep for Christ Jesus,
We'll be a witness for our Lord!**

**We'll write a poem for Christ Jesus,
We'll testify for our Lord!**

**We'll live a life for Christ Jesus,
We'll show love for our Lord!**

**We'll offer all to Christ Jesus,
Give all the credit to our Lord!**

**We'll die a witness for Christ Jesus,
We'll go to glory to live with him!**

Why?

If Christ is Lord,
why don't I crown him king?
If he's the world's creator,
why am I not prostrate?
If he's the Prince of Peace,
let him calm my racing heart.
If he bids me witness,
why don't I bear him fruit?
If he calls me to reconcile,
can't I be his ambassador?
If all derives from him,
can I hold back one thing?
If he's this world's light,
can't I be his reflection?
If God and Son are love,
can't I be love also?
If he's my all in all,
he's all in all in me.

VI

Death at Easter

My dad is dying many miles away—
Azalea buds prepare for birth outside my door;
The second stroke short-circuits his survival hope—
A redbud heralds halt to winter's rule;
His brain, they say, is dulled beyond repair—
The dogwood spots illumine campus green;
His breathing is labored now, they say—
A rainbow arcs from dew on speckled leaves;
The dread report dropped down this late March morn—
Magentan hedge sounds season of new life;
My mother weeps to mate of sixty years—
"Goodbye, I'll see you Resurrection Day."
The grave is sealed on Oklahoma knoll—
But Easter Day is just a lovely bloom away.

Driven

Dedicated to Norman K. Martin

Each day he descends to his basement trove,
there surrounded by PCs that monitor his holdings
stacked in vaults across the globe.
He reads the markets' meanderings,
plots their probable quarterly courses
with singular focus to optimize values,
nudge up all returns,
even amid ailing economies.
He really doesn't need more profits,
in his mansion of many rooms,
children and grandchildren adequately vested.
One passion stokes his furnace,
coals from his Master's lips:
Inasmuch as ye have done it
unto one of the least of these my brethren,
ye have done it unto me. *

*Matthew 25:40

Empty Eyes

If only I could read those empty eyes
that retreat farther day on day,
those pupils fastening on me
from distant shore or alpine pass.
If only I could fathom what you're fixed upon,
eyes that shimmered once like galaxies,
that spoke a language my heart knew,
sometimes turning playfully into a smile.

Are you perchance sorting shared memories
tucked in cerebral folds,
or are synapses hopelessly frayed?
Is there a key rusting beneath a mat—
a pat, a squeeze, a jolt, a sharpened cry?
I pray, oh helping God, just one pontoon
on which to reach those empty eyes.

He's Only Stepped to Another Room

He's only stepped to another room
Whose air is love, whose walls are gold;
All done with pain and dread of tomb,
He's safely in the Savior's fold.

Whose air is love, whose walls are gold,
We cannot mourn his new estate,
He's safely in the Savior's fold,
To meet again our souls must wait.

We cannot mourn his new estate
Where choirs swell in endless praise,
To meet again our souls must wait,
We, too, shall live those glory days.

Where choirs swell in endless praise,
The gathered kneel around the throne;
We, too, shall live those glory days
Secure in perfect final home.

The gathered kneel around the throne,
All done with pain and dread of tomb,
Secure in perfect final home,
He's only stepped to another room.

It Is Enough

It's quite enough this Easter Day
to know he left that stone-cold grave
and that the garden sun's first ray
edged light into deserted cave.

It's quite enough this Easter morn
to recognize the conquest won
o'er death that left his friends forlorn,
now brings them joy with streak of dawn.

It's quite enough in present age
to feel raw power in this deed,
fierce tremors jarred earth's center stage,
and heaven won to cure man's need.

It's quite enough this epic turn
as sin is dealt high remedy,
that people anywhere who yearn
can know forgiveness endlessly.

Sobs

The tiny form decaying in the womb,
devastating to both of us;
and now we sit in our minister's study
for comfort, perhaps understanding.
Years later I can't summon his words,
retrieve the scripture he quoted,
his prayer beyond recall.
Abruptly he falls silent—
I still hear his sobs.

Your Loss

I sense the piercing ache you feel,
Death also dealt its blow to me,
Open wounds, no move to heal,
So many tears I could not see.

Yet life knows how to shrink the pain,
Assuaging myriad rings of grief,
Sunrays glint through dogged rain,
Dispensing doubt with new belief.

The hurt may never seem to leave,
The void may turn into a cross,
But know that ever as you grieve,
I'll circle back to share your loss.

VII

A Giving Heart

Lord, grow in me a giving heart, akin to thine;
a heart which sees others first and service as calling,
a heart which cannot end a day without kindness done,
a heart whose generous spirit is mirrored in my checkbook,
     my calendar, and on the screen of my iphone;
a heart which gives without an eye to status, gender,
     color, creed;
a heart whose concern crosses boundaries, leaps barriers,
     spans oceans, joins families;
a heart with sensors lased toward hurting ones,
a heart that moves me outside myself, shedding the provincial;
a heart reassuring to youth, fostering growth, extending
      horizons;
a heart never lonely because it overflows with people;
a heart which links itself with other giving souls:
hearts with power to drill a well, build a church, rid a disease,
feed the malnourished, calm the troubled, shelter the home-
     less, shield the abused;
a heart which, before it beats its last, will do a universe of good.
Lord, grow in me a giving heart, akin to thine.

AMEN

Bringing Water

Human existence records no nobler deeds than

Bringing water:

> Wets parched lips,
> empowers sanitation,
> recharges body fluids,
> flushes kidneys,
> purges germs,
> sustains animals,
> slakes kids' thirsts,
> fortifies health,
> cleans shirts,
> grows crops.

God's water table,
> cached below surface,
> replenished by clouds,
> eager as young children
> to be tapped
> by people of good will,
> piping hope to people,

Bringing water.

On Foot

In the bottom of the Great Depression
our family of six was on foot,
the four corroded cylinders
of our 1930 Chevrolet having gasped their last.
Like vagrants, we hiked to school, church and store
or caught rides with neighbors.
Then Grandpa died, and we were motoring
across Oklahoma to the funeral
in Reverend Dodson's shiny black sedan.
From the back seat I, age seven,
asked Mom why the preacher
would lend us his prized new vehicle
for us to go bury Pa Lynn.
Mom's reply that morning
was as foggy as lowlands route 70
as we rolled in style toward the church --
something about "a cup of cold water."*

    (Matthew 10:42)*

Remember

When you drink the water,
remember the man who drilled the well.

When you escape the disease,
remember the woman who bought the serum.

When you learn a new truth,
remember the founder of the scholarship.

When your clouded eyes see clearly,
remember the hand positioning the laser.

When you swell to the music,
remember who designed the hearing device.

When you step with the prosthesis,
remember the club which sent it.

When your kids are fed,
remember who shipped the seed.

When your village eats fish,
remember who taught you fish farming.

(Continued)

(Continued)

When you love an organization,
remember who birthed the movement.

When you own a rich heritage,
remember the parents who bequeathed it.

When your thirst is slaked,
remember who piped the water.

When your life is abundant,
remember the creator who grants it all

Service Yields Its Own Rewards

Most will never grasp why we're consumed
with service;
its wages abysmal, its benefits non-existent;
you can't dispense it in any land or time
without sacrifice.
Then why do we adhere to it as life pattern,
adopt it as ever-present passion, appropriate it
as our ideal?
I have discovered that service yields its own rewards,
sows within its selfless actions seeds of joy,
grants enduring nobility to servants of others,
extends to its adherents rare, serendipitous
recompense.

Just knowing that you
helped a person eat, recover, gain dignity, have hope;
enabled crops to grow, water to flow;
helped turn a mere organization into a beacon in a dark world;
etched smiles on kids' faces, toothy grins on old villagers;
spread peace across a hostile globe;
enlarged a mind, handed a boy a future, a girl a life;
brightened a community, cared for her destitute;
built a habitat, mentored a child, clothed a family;
encouraged a youth, built a company, set a legacy;
helped kill a disease, trained young peacemakers;
marching relentlessly toward greatness through servant-hood.

If that bounty won't charge your life's battery,
nothing will.

Someone

Someone mouthed a word of cheer,
Someone scrawled a note of hope,
Someone helped dispel a fear,
Someone led a man to cope,
    Was that someone you?

Someone lent a lifting hand,
Someone filled a neighbor's need,
Someone led a church to stand,
Someone turned a kindly deed,
    Was that someone you?

Someone coached a troubled boy,
Someone drew out lonely girl,
Someone brought him Christmas joy,
Someone sent her her first pearl,
    Was that someone you?

Someone helped a teacher teach,
Someone helped a nurse to nurse,
Someone helped a preacher preach,
Someone helped a child rehearse,
    Was that someone you?

(Continued)

(Continued)

Someone kept a youth in school,
Someone guided child to grow,
Someone taught the Golden Rule,
Someone fanned a mind aglow,
    Was that someone you?

Someone pressed a war to slow,
Someone did a camper send,
Someone made the water flow,
Someone caused disease to end,
    Was that someone you?

Temple Builders

When God desired a temple built
      he anointed Solomon, one of earth's richest;
      the king obeyed, collected prize cedars,
      quarried titanic stones, mined priceless metals,
      and conscripted expert artisans
      to raise Jehovah's construction.

      But now when God needs a new temple
      no Solomon towers over holy real estate
      to manage the daunting enterprise,
      to marshal materials from sea and mount,
      to bind neighbors and enemies for their labor,
      to trade for logs, to hew and set the granite.

      Today a veritable army is mandated to erect a temple,
      a corps of faithful bound by mutual vision
      of spire, worship hall, teaching space, pipes of praise.
      They seldom plumb the walls or trowel the bricks;
      their sweat is a pledge generously vowed, faithfully ful-
filled,
      until in due course God's edifice is consecrated.

    Each giver a Solomon in splendor—
      they blend their prayers with mortar, latex, carpet,
wood,
    while inviting the Master Builder to inhabit the pews,
    the learning halls, the place of sanctuary,
    to foster heaven's purpose as God's workmen
    build his temple and his kingdom.

Yourself a Memorial

How best remember the dead,
three thousand victims of 9-11?
How esteem the perished in twin towers,
airliners made bombers, the Pentagon?

Laud the valor of the fallen
with flowers, verse and gifts,
in tributes, engravings,
letters, songs, and prayers.

But more profoundly: be a memorial yourself.
Vow to be different the rest of your days:
no cowering in terrorism's face,
protecting your own, minimizing risks.

Getting on with your roles,
no stereotyping of others,
reinforcing, replenishing faith,
believing in country, her enduring values.

Sculpt yourself into a memorial,
noble pillar of courage,
granite symbol of human resilience,
tower of hope in dangerous times.

About The Author

Robert L. Lynn took up writing poetry seriously when, as a new college president, he discerned that students of that generation disliked speeches but loved verse. Four hundred poems and over 100 poetry awards later he unveils this collection of spiritual poetry, *Cancer Is So Limited and Other Poems of Faith by Robert L. Lynn.* The book is available at Amazon.com and other retail outlets. The Oklahoma native resides in Duluth, Georgia with his wife, Bonnie. He has written or edited ten books, including two books of poetry, *Service Yields Its Own Rewards* (2007) and *Midnight Verse* (2009). He edited for three years *The Reach of Song,* poetry anthology of the Georgia Poetry Society. He is also a member of statewide poetry societies in Oklahoma and Alabama. Dr. Lynn's poems have been published in numerous publications and journals. The author founded the Johns Creek Poetry Group in Atlanta and reads his poetry an average of twenty times a year to adult and youth audiences across the Southeastern United States. Hear him read his poetry at www.robertllynn.com For permissions and scheduling contact: robertllynn@comcast.net

Made in the USA
Charleston, SC
24 August 2013